Hear Ye of Philadelphia

Hear Ye

Lothrop, Lee & Shepard Co., Inc., New York

# of Philadelphia

by POLLY CURREN

pictures by KURT WERTH

I can still remember how confused I was when I first began to study American history. There was so much going on in so many places—and all at the same time. So I decided to choose one place and write a book telling only what happened there, and then move on to other places and describe events happening at the same time *there*—until I had told the entire story of how our nation began and grew.

I started my story with Boston—which you can read about in *Hear Ye of Boston*—and now we've come to Philadelphia, the City of Brotherly Love, where our nation was born.

Polly Curren

Philadelphia is
a great and famous city—
a quiet and friendly, neat and orderly
voice-of-freedom city.
This is Philadelphia.

Her streets are wide and very straight,
and some of them are named for the trees that
used to grow there.

Right in the middle of old Philadelphia,
where Broad Street crosses Market,
is City Hall. High on its rooftop
a statue of William Penn looks out over his city.
And way down on Chestnut Street, in Independence Square,
is the old red-brick State House,
now called Independence Hall.

Ocean liners and freight ships are tied up at
the docks that line the wide Delaware River.
And tall dark smokestacks—and round fat oil tanks—
poke up into the air.

Trucks and buses move along the crowded streets.
The railroads and highways are busy with traffic,
and the airport is noisy with planes.
And this is Philadelphia today.
But long ago, it was very different.

Philadelphia was founded almost three hundred years
ago by a young Englishman named William Penn.
He belonged to a religious group, the Society of Friends
(called Quakers), who were very unpopular in England
because they truly believed that all men were equal, and
because they were against war and refused to take oaths
of any kind.
One day in 1681, William Penn went to King Charles
and asked for land in America as payment of a debt
the King owed William Penn's father. He wanted to find a
new home for his people. King Charles gave him a large
grant of land, rich with green woodlands, and the Quakers
named it Pennsylvania—which means "Penn's Woods."

In the autumn of 1682, William Penn
and some of his Quaker friends came to Pennsylvania
on the ship *Welcome,* and made their new home where
the Schuylkill and Delaware Rivers meet.

One of the first things William Penn did was to meet
with the Indians and promise them friendship
for "as long as the sun gives light."
Some people say Penn made this promise under a
giant elm tree—called "The Treaty Elm."

Then Penn and his Quakers went to work and began to
build their town—the "greene countrie towne."
They laid out the streets straight and wide, and crisscrossed
them in a neat checkerboard fashion.
They planted farmlands with grain, and fruit, and
vegetables. And they began to raise cattle
and pigs and sheep.

They cleared the rivers and made a fine harbor, and they
built a shipyard beside the wide Delaware.
They cut down the tall trees of the forest and
built strong ships to sail the seas.
Before long small neat houses, some of brick and some
of stone, lined the streets that led from the river.

More people came from England to join the Friends in the New World. When the Quaker city was only two years old there were six hundred houses in Philadelphia.

There were grist mills to grind the grain into flour. There was a paper mill on Paper Mill Creek. There was a printing press—the only one between Boston and Mexico City.

There were weavers who made fine linen and
linsey-woolsey cloth. There were leather workers
who made shoes and saddles and harnesses from hides and
skins.

Then iron was discovered, and great forges were built to
make all kinds of iron products—more than were needed
in Philadelphia.

So the surplus was loaded onto ships,
along with farm products, and sent over to
England, and down the coast, and off to the West Indies.
And the ships brought back wealth and luxuries.
Churches were built, not just for the Quakers
but for all faiths—and there was religious
freedom for everybody.
Philadelphia grew and grew, and her people
were busy and happy.

One day in 1723 a young man from Boston
came to live in Philadelphia.
His name was Benjamin Franklin.
He published Philadelphia's first real newspaper, the
Gazette, in 1729.
He opened America's first circulating library in 1731,
and he helped found America's first hospital in 1751.
He also founded the school that later became the
University of Pennsylvania.
Ben Franklin was the one who thought of the first
paved streets and the first street lights and the
first night watchmen in America. He was a leading citizen
in a time of growth and prosperity for Philadelphia.
But there was trouble ahead.

George the Third, King of England, needed money to
support his homeland and his growing armies.
Some of his soldiers had been sent to America to help protect
the colonists from warring Indians and from the action of
unfriendly French soldiers who were in Canada.
King George knew his American colonies were wealthy,
and he wanted them to help pay for their own protection.
So the King and his Parliament passed the Stamp Act,
putting a tax on all paper and documents.
Then they passed the Townshend Acts and taxed almost
everything that came into and went out of all harbors.
The colonists had had no voice in these laws—
and they felt that the taxes were wrong.
In every one of the colonies the people refused to buy
the stamps. With all the colonies united against it,
King George and Parliament had to repeal the Stamp Act
and part of the Townshend Acts in 1766.
But they left the tax on tea.
And Philadelphia, just like Boston and the other cities,
refused to buy any tea sent by England.

It was Paul Revere who rode from Boston, in December of 1773, to bring Philadelphia the news of the Boston Tea Party. He told the people how some Boston patriots had stolen aboard British ships anchored in Boston Harbor and how they had thrown the cargo of tea into the water.

And when spring came, Paul Revere rode again
to Philadelphia with the news that King George,
instead of listening to the colonists, had closed
the port of Boston.
When Pennsylvania and the other colonies heard how the
King was punishing the people of Boston, the colonists
were afraid that he might take away the privileges and
freedom they had gained in America.
The time had come to stand up for the rights
they believed to be theirs.

That September over fifty men came to Philadelphia
from every colony, except Georgia.
They met in Carpenters' Hall and they talked over all the
things that made them unhappy—the heavy taxes, the
governors' salaries, the many things that the King forbade
them to do, and the things that he ordered them to do.
Then they wrote out a petition asking King George to be
fair and to give them back their just rights as Englishmen.

The King refused.
So they asked all the people in all the colonies to
stop buying anything from England, and to stop sending
England anything from America.
But no one at that meeting said one single word about
wanting to be independent from England, their motherland.
That was the First Continental Congress.

As time went on the colonists grew more upset
and uneasy. British soldiers in Boston watched the
people there very carefully. And the people in
Pennsylvania and the other colonies watched Boston—
and worried and waited to see what would happen.

Then, on the 19th of April, in 1775, British soldiers and
some Boston Minutemen fought each other at
Concord and Lexington. This was the first battle
of the American Revolution, and
news of the fighting spread like wildfire.
The delegates to the First Continental Congress
came back to Philadelphia for a second meeting.
This time they met in the State House.
All of them were worried, and a few of them were angry
and dared to whisper a wish for independence.
But most of them wanted only to find a way to
remain loyal to their King.
They wrote another petition and sent it to King George,
but they got ready to fight, if necessary, to
protect their rights. They named
George Washington their General, and made him
Commander-in-Chief of the American soldiers.

That was the Second Continental Congress.

Day by day the trouble grew worse.
And one year later, in June, 1776, this same
Second Continental Congress—still in session in
Philadelphia's State House—took action.
They decided the time had come for the colonies
to declare themselves free and independent of England.
Thomas Jefferson, from Virginia,
wrote their Declaration of Independence.
And two other men, John Hancock, President of the
Congress, and Charles Thomson, the Secretary, signed
the paper—on the 4th of July in 1776.

Four days later the Declaration was read to the crowds
gathered in the State House yard.
The people cheered and shouted with joy.
And the great iron bell in the tower—now called
the Liberty Bell—rang out the news.

King George replied to the Declaration of Independence
by sending more British troops. The fighting grew
worse, and men from every colony marched off to war.
Now Philadelphia's factories made gunpowder, and her
shipyards built warships.

In September, 1777, Philadelphia was captured by the
British. That winter British officers moved into the finest
homes in Philadelphia, and enjoyed warm fires and good
food. They went to the theaters and danced at gay balls.
Sometimes they practiced their shooting and used the
weather vane on top of Carpenters' Hall for their target.

Just outside the city, that same winter, General George
Washington and his ragged army camped at
Valley Forge. They had little to eat, and their naked
feet left footprints of blood in the snow. But
they never lost courage and were ready
when the time for battle came.

At last, in 1781, after long and bitter fighting,
the war was over.
The French fleet had been sent to help Washington
and his brave, weary army
and together they had trapped the British.
Far to the south of Philadelphia
in the small village of Yorktown, in Virginia,
Lord Cornwallis, the gallant British commander,
surrendered his army to General George Washington.

America had won her independence!

Now Philadelphia became the chief city of America.
In 1787, the Constitution of the United States was drawn
up and signed in the red-brick State House
now famous as Independence Hall. Philadelphia
became the first capital of the new nation.
George Washington, the first President, lived there.
The first United States Congress met there.
The first Supreme Court sat there.
The first Mint, which made the first American money,
and the first Navy Yard to build American ships,
were there.
Philadelphia was a proud city.

In the nineteenth century many people from the old lands
in Europe came to live in the Quaker city. They brought
with them new ideas, new plans, great ambitions, and
the determination to work hard to achieve them.

New machines were invented, and more factories were
built, to make clothing, and carpets and paper
and all kinds of iron goods, from
small nails to giant machines.
And when railroads were built, Philadelphia began
to build locomotives.

The city of Philadelphia was called "The Workshop
of the World."

In 1876, there was a big celebration in Philadelphia
in honor of 100 years of independence.
It was called the "Centennial Exposition."
Five great halls were built in Fairmount Park and filled
with the best and newest American inventions.
Bell's telephone, a giant steam engine, works of art,
man-made products, and products of the land were there.

All the nations of the world were invited to come to
America's one hundredth birthday party.
This was the first World's Fair.
Nine million, nine hundred thousand people from all over
America and all over the world came to see it.

After the Centennial Exposition, more writers and poets
and artists began coming to live in Philadelphia,
and an art museum and symphony orchestra
were founded.
Philadelphia, which had always prospered, was now one
of the richest, as well as one of the most cultured
cities in America.

Philadelphia's schools and colleges grew more famous,
and her medical schools and hospitals—the oldest
in America—were known all over the world.
By the end of the nineteenth century there were
fifteen times more people in Philadelphia
than at the beginning of that century.

In the twentieth century, constantly growing,
Philadelphia has built a fine airport and wide superhighways.
The old houses that were worn out and useless have been
torn down. Streets that had grown crowded and ugly
have been replanned, but the layout of the streets
is still as William Penn designed it.
New apartments and houses are being
built so that Philadelphia's people can live better.

The old sites and buildings, where history
was made, were never destroyed. They are being restored
and made to look as they had in bygone days.

Philadelphians are proud of their history, and of the places where that history was made: Independence Square with its row of neat red-brick buildings; Independence Hall, where our nation was born; the Assembly Room, where the Constitution was signed; and especially the Liberty Bell—the voice of freedom—that rang out the news in the quiet Quaker-town of Philadelphia when the Declaration of Independence was first proclaimed.

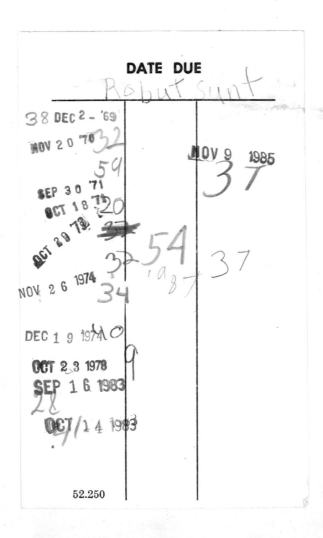

DATE DUE

Robert sunt

38 DEC 2 - '69

NOV 20 '70 32

59

SEP 30 '71

OCT 18 73 20

OCT 29 73

NOV 26 1974 32 54

34 37

DEC 1 9 1974 0

9

OCT 2 3 1978

SEP 1 6 1983

28

OCT 1 4 1983

NOV 9 1985

37